Woody the Woodlouse
who forgot how to roll into a ball

by Sonia Copeland Bloom

With illustrations by Nick Page

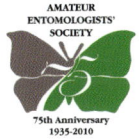

This first edition is published by
The Amateur Entomologists' Society 2011
Registered Charity No. 267430
PO Box 8774, London SW7 5ZG
www.amentsoc.org

© Sonia Copeland Bloom 2010
The Author asserts her moral rights to be identified
as the author of this work.
All rights reserved.

This book is sponsored by the Betty Copeland legacy.
*All proceeds from this edition will support the work of the
Amateur Entomologists' Society*

Printed by: Design & Print Centre, University of Kent
Email: print_office@kent.ac.uk

Page layouts by Darren Gander Graphic Design
Email: darren.gander@talktalk.net

*Woodlouse photos ©Paul Richards,
www.invertebrate-images.co.uk*

ISBN 978-0-900054-78-5

EDITORIAL FOREWORD

In this, the second in a series of 'faction' books by Sonia Copeland Bloom, the author's audacious new approach to engaging children with the natural world is applied to life in the undergrowth and leaf litter, where woodlice and other tiny creatures live.

Utilising a careful mix of fact and fiction, a captivating tale about a woodlouse is complemented by salient facts about these tiny crustaceans and other invertebrates.

There is also a glossary of carefully selected 'technical' words for young readers. These are highlighted in bold in the text from page 6 onwards when first encountered. There is also a section that gives advice on keeping woodlice as pets.

This innovative series represents a new departure for the society, which has traditionally published non-fiction titles aimed at the amateur entomologist. Gratifyingly, much interest was shown in the first book in the series – *Basil the Beetle's Scary Adventure* – by schools as well as by children and their parents. This endorsement has renewed our hope that the series will spark a new interest in natural history among the young people who will ultimately be responsible for the future of our world.

Dafydd Lewis
Hon. Secretary, Amateur Entomologists' Society

THE AMATEUR ENTOMOLOGISTS' SOCIETY

Founded in 1935, the Amateur Entomologists' Society is a leading society for anyone interested in insects and their natural history. Its primary aim is to promote the study of entomology, especially amongst amateurs and the younger generation, through the publication of books and periodicals and the organisation of educational events.

AUTHOR'S PREFACE

There has never been such an urgent need to engage more young people with natural history. This second book in the series *Tales and Truths about Garden Minibeasts* has been produced swiftly on the heels of the first because of the enthusiastic response to *Basil the Beetle's Scary Adventure* and the appreciation of the series concept in general: that is, to present a new and active way to engage children with the natural world.

So here comes Woody, a kind-hearted woodlouse whose own problems were solved by doing a brave favour for a spider – who, I suppose, could have gobbled him up but instead became a lifelong friend!

Having access to a subject through our emotions as we read or listen to a story has an important place alongside the absorption of pure facts. The anthropomorphic aspects of each story are there to encourage the growth of genuine affection and wonder in young children for the incredible miracles of the world of invertebrates.

Never mind that our minibeast hero and his friends actually *talk* to each other, occasionally *shed a tear* and *do favours* for their families and friends! To encourage our youngsters to put on gumboots for a dose of fresh air so they can find and fall in love with a beetle, a woodlouse, a little caterpillar, a slimy slug, and a wiggling worm (all stories in the pipeline) may produce an experience which could forever stamp a sympathetic memory on their fast-developing minds.

*Dedicated to
the memory of Betty Copeland*

and to Savannah King

CONTENTS

Editorial foreword 3
Author's preface 4
Woody the Woodlouse who forgot how to roll into a ball 6
The Hornby family and their garden 22
Glossary of important words 24
The wonderful world of woodlice 26
Fascinating facts about minibeasts 28
Keeping woodlice as pets is fun 29
Where to go for more information 30
Acknowledgements 35

*Words that appear in the Glossary are highlighted in **bold**
the first time they appear in the book from page 6 onwards.*

5

Woody the Woodlouse
who forgot how to roll into a ball

A common pill-bug woodlouse.

How much do you know about woodlice?

You can find these smart little creatures hiding underneath a large stone, a rock or log in your garden where they make their homes. In the countryside they live under damp leaves and in rotting tree trunks. Warm, dry weather doesn't suit them at all. They hide during the day and come out at night when it's cool and damp. There are many different types and colours of **woodlice** but all of them have segmented bodies with interlocking coats like armour – most often slate-grey in colour.

Some kinds of woodlice can conveniently roll into a tight ball if they want to protect themselves from danger. Like many other creepy crawlies, woodlice shed their coats as they grow larger after first growing a brand new one underneath.

At sunset and once darkness has fallen, the woodlice come out in their hordes to feed and play. Woodlouse mothers are considered to be among the best in the whole of the **minibeast** world!
They have large families and care for them well, so they grow up in a happy family and are seldom lonely.

But this is a story about Woody, a special woodlouse who became sad *and* lonely, until he did a good turn for a friend…

CHAPTER ONE

W oody the woodlouse lived with his father and mother, and his many brothers and sisters, aunts, uncles and grandparents, under a large rock in the garden of the Hornby family who live at 6 Maple Way.

The woodlice's home was part of a rock garden. Covered with colourful plants, it provided a safe shelter for the woodlice — who, as you know, are very small creatures.

Being such a close family, the woodlice looked out for each other. The parents often reminded their young not to stray too far from home. They knew that some of their neighbours, especially hedgehogs, shrews and frogs, were partial to woodlouse stew!

Pa and Ma Woodlouse, as they were known, spent a great deal of their time gathering food with their large family. Everyone joined in the search for **leaf litter** which they turned into a tasty feast, mixed with favourite treats such as scraps of vegetables or fruit.

Woody enjoyed life with his friends and family. Like all woodlice, he had seven pairs of legs and loved to scurry in and around the garden, exploring and playing. His shiny coat was made up of interlocking segments, allowing him to roll into a ball.

Woody could squeeze into the tiniest nooks and crannies in the garden, which was useful when playing hide and seek. In the morning, the woodlice returned home to rest throughout the day in the dampness under the rocks.

One night, Woody found a perfect place to hide under a piece of broken flower pot. He prepared, as usual, to curl up into a ball. But this time, when he tried to roll up his body, the steel-grey segments of his coat refused to budge.

He tried again and again, but each time he ended up doing a clumsy somersault, landing on his back, feeling foolish with his little legs waving in the air.

"Come on, Woody, it's your turn now," said his brothers and sisters, puzzled that it was taking Woody so long to hide. But it was no good - Woody could not roll himself up!

He could run around without tripping over his fourteen legs. But turning into a ball now seemed impossible for Woody. The others did all they could to help but each time he tried, he landed on his back and soon they gave up.

The next day, Woody tried again, but the same thing happened. Pa and Ma Woodlouse became very worried. Their family had always been able to roll into a ball: it was how they protected themselves when they were frightened. Everyone took it in turns to inspect Woody's coat.
They rubbed him all over with dew drops mixed with Ma's special lotion for stomach aches, but with no success.

Armadillidium depressum

Woody became sadder and more lonely as his brothers and sisters reluctantly gave up playing with him. Ma Woodlouse gave him plenty of hugs.

"Don't leave him out of your games," she told the family. "We try not to, Ma," they said. "But Woody's not much fun to play with now."

CHAPTER TWO

One day Woody decided to go off on his own for a long walk. He felt that if he was left in peace, he might remember how to roll himself into a ball again.

On and on he tramped through the woods. Occasionally, his **antennae** would smell a tasty snack, which he would chew to keep up his strength.

Then, in the east of the sky, a tiny ray of light appeared. Night was nearly over. Woody looked around him. Which way was home? he wondered.

Everything seemed to be going from bad to worse for the little woodlouse. First, he could no longer roll into a ball, and now he was lost. He felt very sad and alone. Would he ever get back to his family?

Suddenly, he heard a voice calling, "Help me, help me!" Woody looked left and right, in front and behind him, but he couldn't see anyone.

"Help me, help me!" the voice cried again.

The sound seemed to be coming from above him. He turned onto his back and looked upwards. What was that dangling from a branch of a tree just above him?

It was Spinny the **Spider**! Woody was so pleased to see Spinny that he immediately stopped feeling lonely.

"What's up Spinny?" he said.

"Oh, it's you Woody. I didn't recognize you lying on your back like that. My, you are a long way from home for a short-legged woodlouse!" exclaimed the spider.

"Yes, I'm in trouble. I think I've lost my way!" sighed Woody. "Ever since I forgot how to roll into a ball things have gone wrong, and now no one will play with me."

"I've got a serious problem too," said the spider.

"What's the matter Spinny?" asked Woody with concern.

"You'd never believe it," replied Spinny. "I've run out of my silken thread. It's never happened before. I thought I would go exploring but here I am, stuck in the air. I don't know what to do."

Woody could see Spinny's eight long legs dangling and swinging in the air.

"What's more," continued Spinny, "the birds are tuning up for the dawn chorus - any minute now, one of them will come along and gobble me up for breakfast!" Spinny looked around. Being a spider, he had many eyes in his head so he could see all around himself without moving.

"Oh dear," said Woody in dismay. "Can't you bend your legs just a little and then jump?"

"My legs have been dangling for so long that it's difficult to move them," replied Spinny.

Spinny suddenly swung himself sideways. "Help!" he cried out in alarm. "That blackbird nearly got me!"

He looked downwards. Spinny was used to climbing down from trees with the help of his strong **silk** thread, so he was not usually afraid of heights. Without being able to use his thread he looked down nervously. "If I jump down, I'm sure to crush my legs!"

"It's a long way down," agreed Woody. "What can we do? If only I could roll into a ball, I could go for help quickly."

Then he had an idea.

"Listen Spinny! Why don't I build a large pile of leaves for you to fall on? I could build a stack of leaves so high - like a tower, so you wouldn't feel you had too far to fall!"

"What a clever idea!" said Spinny, hopeful that Woody might save him.

CHAPTER THREE

Woody got busy immediately, gathering up leaves and putting them one on top of another until they made a pile underneath where Spinny was dangling from a tree. He felt hot, working so hard. Then he noticed that his coat seemed to have torn in half!

It had fallen onto the ground in two pieces. He felt alarmed - what would his mother say! Then he turned his head and saw that a new shiny coat had replaced the old one!

"My!" he thought with pride, thinking about his new coat as he clambered to the top of the tower of leaves he had made for Spinny to fall onto, dragging the last leaf behind him.

"That's a smart new coat!" said Spinny admiringly from above. "But hurry please, Woody - the new day is dawning and there are some hungry birds looking for food so we haven't much time."

He peered down. "It still seems a long way to jump!" he said with a note of panic in his voice.

"Listen Spinny," said Woody. "If I lie on my back on the pile of leaves, with all my legs in the air, you could bounce onto me for a soft landing as if I were a trampoline!"

"Another good idea! Woody - you are an amazing friend!" said Spinny.

Woody climbed to the top of the leaf tower and, once there, lay down on his back and stretched out his legs. Then he called out - "Get ready to jump Spinny!"

The spider looked down fearfully. A nasty buzz from a wasp and a hungry twitter from a pair of starlings made him realise it was now or never!

"OK Woody? Ready... steady... go!"

Spinny broke the thread that fastened him to the branch. He didn't look down, but jumped and hoped for the best.

He fell onto Woody's fourteen little legs which made a bouncy landing for him.

"Phew, that was a close one. Thank you so much Woody!"

The two creatures climbed down from the leaf pile. They felt so relieved to be safe that they gave each other a hug. Spinny's long legs tickled Woody's tummy so much, Woody got the giggles.

He giggled and giggled and giggled. He giggled so much that he doubled up into a little ball. Spinny started laughing too. He laughed so much that his legs also folded up beneath him.

Woody's new coat helped him to curl up extra tight. He stopped laughing for a moment.

"Look what's happened Spinny! I've remembered how to roll into a ball!"

The spider was happy for Woody. Then he looked down at his own legs. "And my legs are now working perfectly! Both of our problems have gone - all because we helped each other!"

They had a long walk home and so Spinny suggested that Woody should turn himself into a ball. Then Spinny used his long legs to roll Woody all the way back to the garden at 6 Maple Way!

The friends and family of the two little creatures turned out to greet them, pleased that they had solved their problems and were safely back home.

Pa and Ma Woodlouse were delighted to see Woody looking so happy. They quickly prepared a spread of tasty food and drink so that everyone could enjoy a welcome home party in the garden.

Then Woody's popular Woodlice Big Band, made up of his brothers, sisters and friends, appeared in a musical procession. They banged their daisy drums, jingled bluebells and blew hard on their golden cowslip trumpets.

For the rest of their lives, Woody and Spinny remained the best of friends.

A Woodlouse   *by Stani (aged 9)*

My hero is a woodlouse because
How swiftly they tuck and roll;
How brilliantly they dodge your stamping rampaging feet;
How intelligently they scuttle about looking for moss.
Because how defensive they can be when dropping from great heights;
How kindly they offer food to fellow ants;
How fabulously they hide in shelter;
How bravely they face whole termite armies just for a single crumb.
Because how fantastically they jump *just* out of reach of human hands,
                    waiting to crush like a machine;
How marvellously they twist their way out of a waiting spider's web;
How magically….
How wonderfully…
    …Just woodlice!

by Estanislao 'Stani' Miles, aged 9,
from the Little Green Pig writing project.
This poem won the East Sussex County Council's 2010
'Heroes and Heroines' poetry competition.

THE HORNBY FAMILY AND THEIR GARDEN

All the stories in the Tales and Truths Series about Garden Minibeasts take place in the garden of Mr and Mrs Hornby and their children, Thomas, aged seven, Hugo, just six, and little Lizzie who is three and three-quarters. They live at 6 Maple Way and their home and garden are situated just outside the town centre, with a park nearby and not too far from the countryside.

The Hornbys enjoy their garden. They play games out there in the fresh air. Early in the year, they look out for the appearance of snowdrops in the garden, then crocuses and daffodils that herald spring. They enjoy sowing flower and vegetable seeds, watching them grow around the garden, or in tidy rows in the 'veg' patch behind the garden shed. They all agree there is something very special about eating new potatoes, carrots, beans, tomatoes and lettuces that they have grown themselves - without using nasty chemicals - picked fresh from the garden.

Beside the vegetable patch is a compost heap, where unwanted remains of plants can be put. The compost serves as a cosy home to many small creatures, and can also be dug into the earth to enrich the soil.

The Hornbys love to watch the garden birds that feed at their bird table, especially in winter when food is scarce. Sometimes a green woodpecker with a bright red head visits the garden, to feed on ants in the lawn.

They especially like to see the activities of the tiniest creatures in the garden. Some of them live in a pile of rotting logs which Mr Hornby leaves out especially for them. The wild flower patch is a favourite with bees, hoverflies and butterflies, and the small garden pond (covered with wire netting for safety) is home to many **insects**, such as dragonflies and pond skaters, as well as newts and frogs.

In the shelter of a tree in the Hornbys' garden is a bundle of short bamboo canes, inside an old piece of pipe, where bees and lacewings live, and **hibernate**. The children call it their '**minibeast hotel**'!

Little Lizzie, especially, loves to search for ladybirds on the roses or hedges. They are all delighted when they find a **caterpillar**. As long as they make sure they find the plant it likes to feed from (caterpillars tend to eat only certain leaves), they like to take the caterpillar inside to look after it as a pet in a specially prepared box. The children eagerly wait for it to turn into a **chrysalis**. Weeks later it breaks out, like a miracle, into a butterfly or moth.

Gardens are fun places to explore and learn from, and even very small gardens are teeming with minibeasts. Even if you do not have a garden, you could make your own minibeast hotel, or grow some lavender, mint or other herbs in pots by the door or on the window ledge of your home.

Left to right: Mrs Hornby, Hugo, little Lizzie, Thomas and Mr Hornby.

Activity ideas

- *Could you draw a picture of your garden or a favourite wild place?*
- *Write a description of 'a secret garden' and list all the wildlife you would like to discover there.*
- *Write a poem about a favourite garden minibeast that you have observed in your garden or in the countryside.*
- *Make a list of some of the flowers and trees that often grow in gardens or parks. You could also draw and paint the flowers and the leaves of the trees you choose.*

GLOSSARY

Try finding these words in bold print, all special to the study of insects, within the pages of this book.

* **Antennae:** These are the 'feelers' on the head of an **insect**. They are sensory organs – the animals use them to 'feel' and smell their surroundings.

* **Arthropod:** Arthropods are **invertebrate** animals that have a jointed skeleton, on the outside of their bodies. Examples of arthropods include **crustaceans** (such as crabs and lobsters, and of course woodlice) as well as **spiders** and **insects**.

* **Bee box:** Bee boxes are usually a bunch of short hollow pieces of bamboo inside a sheltered, protective box that is open on one side. Bees and other insects can nest, hide or hibernate in them, in the garden.

* **Bug:** The word 'bug' when used by **entomologists** can mean a particular kind of insect (in the **Order** Hemiptera). The word is also sometimes used for other things completely, such as a 'computer bug' (computer problem) or an infection (such as the common cold)!

* **Caterpillar:** see **larva**.

* **Chrysalis:** see **pupa**.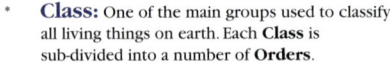

* **Class:** One of the main groups used to classify all living things on earth. Each **Class** is sub-divided into a number of **Orders**.

* **Classification:** This refers to how we describe all living things on earth and how they are related. There are seven main levels of classification in all.

  The first four, starting with the broadest are:

  Kingdom (e.g. Animal or Plant kingdom);

  Phylum (such as the Arthropoda);

  Class (such as the Insects);

  Order (such as the **Isopoda** (woodlice) or the Lepidoptera (butterflies and moths).

  Each Order is then divided into Families, and within each Family, every animal belongs to a **Genus** and a **Species** according to the way it looks and behaves. (In the Plant Kingdom, the word 'Division' is used instead of 'Phylum').

* **Compound eyes:** Most insects have eyes made up of a number of individual 'mini-eyes', also known as ommatidia. The world looks very different through their eyes!

* **Crustaceans:** Crustaceans are a large group of **arthropod** animals. Most live in fresh water or sea water, and well known ones are crabs, lobsters and shrimps. However, woodlice, which live on land, are crustaceans too.

* **Entomology:** Entomology is the study of insects. Someone who studies insects is called an entomologist.

*A **bee-box** in the garden can help attract insects.*
Image ©Phil Wilkins

* **Food chain:** This describes the 'chain' of living things from which energy (mainly from sunlight) is passed to power most life on earth. The chain is made up of **predators** and prey (prey is what predators eat). Plants use the energy in sunlight to make stored energy, in the form of sugars. The plants may then be eaten by minibeasts, such as caterpillars or woodlice. They, in turn, may be eaten by garden birds, spiders or other small animals. These animals may then be eaten by larger ones, and so it goes on, up the chain to lions and to man, who are at the top of the food chain.

* **Fossil:** Fossils are traces or remains of animals and plants that lived thousands or even millions of years ago. They can be found in rocks, including in quarries or on the beach.

* **Genus:** A genus is one of the main groups used to classify all living things on earth. Each genus contains a number of species. (See also **Classification**).

* **Habitat:** An area with the particular environmental conditions that an animal needs to live.

* **Hibernate:** In winter some animals, including many minibeasts, go into hibernation. When they hibernate, their growth, development and all activity stops, until the winter is over and they 'wake up' in the spring.

24

* **Insects:** Insects are the largest Class of **arthropods**, and the most diverse group of animals in the world. They make up around 8 out of every 10 animal species.

* **Invertebrate:** This is an animal without a backbone. Invertebrates make up 95% of all animal species.

* **Isopoda:** This is the **Order** of animals that woodlice belong to.

* **Larva:** The juvenile form of many insects, which looks very different from the adult. Larvae of butterflies and moths are also known as caterpillars. A fly larva is called a maggot.

* **Leaf litter:** This is dead plant material, made from the leaves that have fallen from trees in the autumn. Leaf litter is often home to minibeasts, such as woodlice and insects.

* **Metamorphosis:** Some insects, such as flies, beetles and butterflies, **moult** through distinct stages, with an abrupt change between each stage. This is called complete metamorphosis. In these insects, each egg hatches into a **larva**, which looks very different from its parents. The larva grows by shedding its skin. The fully grown larva then goes into a sleeping stage, known as a **pupa** which eventually sheds its skin to become the adult beetle, fly or butterfly. When there is no pupal stage (for example in dragonflies and stick insects) that is called incomplete metamorphosis.

* **Minibeast:** The name given to any small creature, usually an **invertebrate**, such as an **insect** or a **woodlouse**. Minibeasts are also sometimes called '**bugs**' or 'creepy-crawlies'. Minibeasts are often described as cold-blooded because they are usually the same temperature as their surroundings and therefore tend to be more active when it is warm. Some insects can, however, warm themselves up by sunning themselves or by vibrating their wing muscles.

* **Minibeast hotel:** see **Bee box**.

* **Moulting:** Woodlice and other arthropods grow by shedding their outer protective skeletons. First, a new skeleton forms underneath the old one. The inner part of the old skeleton then dissolves, leaving a thin outer 'skin', which is discarded. The new skeleton is puffed up and hardens.

* **Order:** An Order is one of the main groups used for classification of all living things on earth.

* **Pollen:** Pollen grains contain the male cells of flowers. They merge with the female cells of flowers to form the fertile seeds.

* **Pollination:** This is the process by which **pollen** is transferred from one plant to another. This can be by wind, or by being carried by small animals who visit the flowers for nectar or pollen.

* **Predators:** A predator is an animal which eats other animals. Many insects are predatory, for example praying mantids and dragonflies. These insects are often active during the day, and they have large **compound eyes** to allow them to spot their prey. Other well known invertebrate predators include spiders. Predators and prey make up the links in the **food chain**.

* **Pupa:** A pupa is the sleeping stage of an insect, which eventually moults and becomes the adult stage. The pupa of a butterfly is often called a **chrysalis**. In some insects, the pupa is protected inside a shell (such as a cocoon made of silk).

* **Silk:** Silk is a strong thread which spiders and some insects (such as the silkworm moth) can make. Spiders can spin it into a web to catch prey, and they can make a nest from it. They can also spin it and hang from it as they move from branch to branch in a tree or bush.

* **Species:** A species is a group of organisms that can breed and produce fertile offspring. The name of each species is always written as the name of the Genus it belongs to (with the first letter in capitals) followed by its own specific name (beginning with a lower case letter). For example, *Porcellio scaber* is the common garden woodlouse, belonging to the Genus *Porcellio*.

* **Spider:** An Order of arthropods. One way that spiders are different from their cousins, the insects, is by having eight legs (insects have only six). Spiders are known for the webs they weave from silk.

* **Woodlouse:** A type of small land-dwelling **crustacean**.

For further information on these words, and to look up hundreds of other entomology terms, you can check out the online glossary compiled by the AES.
www.amentsoc.org/insects/glossary

The Wonderful World of Woodlice

Woodlice have been around on earth for millions of years, as scientists have discovered from **fossils** found in rocks. They used to live in the sea, but some 50 million years ago these little creatures walked onto the land and found they could live there, as long as they stayed in damp, cool places. After all this time, things haven't changed: they still like to hide in dark, damp places. It may seem strange but the little woodlice you can find in your garden are related to animals that look quite different. These include crabs, shrimps and lobsters which, of course, live in the sea. They all belong to a big group called **Crustaceans**.

There are an amazing 3500 types of woodlice around the world. The funny names they can be called include: slaters, sow bugs, pill bugs, roly-polies, chiggy-pigs, bibble bugs and fairies' pigs! Some of these names are used because certain species can roll into a ball-like form when threatened by **predators**, leaving only their armoured backs exposed.

Woodlice are food for larger animals, such as hedgehogs and shrews, but there are some spiders, known as woodlouse spiders (you can find one on page 36), that do eat woodlice. Of course, these spiders are not the same kind as Spinny in the story in this book!

Too many people feel that woodlice are pests and want to kill them. This is a pity, because woodlice are actually useful for helping to enrich garden soil. Woodlice hatch from eggs which the mother carries in a pouch. The pouch contains a food supply for the baby woodlice which stay there for quite a long time before they are ready to be released. Woodlice mothers are very caring of their young and are considered to be one of the best mothers among garden minibeasts.

Like Woody, all woodlice have segmented bodies and seven pairs of jointed legs. However, when they are first hatched, they only have six pairs – the last pair appears when they start moulting. Moulting is what happens when a woodlouse sheds its coat. Woodlice are unique among the **arthropods** in moulting in two halves. Before that happens, a new coat begins to grow underneath the old one. The old coat is shed in two halves, as you can see from the drawing of Woody on page 16 and in the second photo on the top of the inside front cover. The shiny, clean new coat is soft at first and the woodlouse puffs it up to make it larger than the old one before it hardens.

Woodlice have eyes, but they are not like yours and mine. Their eyes are made up of lots of smaller eyes bundled together to form what is known as a **compound eye**. Woodlouse mouthparts are very different from ours and can't form an actual smile. Because their mouths are fairly weak, they can only eat soft food - such as decaying plants and leaves or, occasionally, young seedlings.

Their pair of sensitive antennae or feelers are important to them, as they use them to find the best place to live, to look for food and to find a suitable mate. Pill woodlice like Woody live for up to four years.

Land-living woodlice evolved from seawater crustaceans.
Ligea oceanica *is a species of woodlouse that has evolved to go back to the sea.*

Fascinating Facts about Minibeasts

Many children are interested in minibeasts. They can be seen in gardens, under rocks and leaves, or crawling, flying or buzzing around. Their lives are spent busily searching for food, and avoiding being eaten by other small animals in the neighbourhood, who are also constantly on the lookout for a tasty bite.

Did you know that the world as we know it could not exist without the important work of insects and other **invertebrates** (as animals that do not have backbones are called)?

Insects are very important animals. For one thing, 8 out of 10 **species** of all living things in the world are insects! Insects are vital for **pollination** of crops, trees and wild flowers. Without them, many crops would fail and lots of our common foods would disappear. Can you imagine a world without the tiny fly that pollinates the cocoa plant? Without it, there would be no chocolate!

Burying beetles dig underneath dead animals and cover them in soil, so that the bodies decompose and provide food for the beetle **larvae**. If they didn't do this, our gardens and the countryside would be knee deep in dead animals! Woodlice do the same with dead or decaying plants - they eat them, and then recycle them as nutrients back into the soil. Underground, the tilling work of worms mixes the soil, helping air, moisture and the roots of plants to spread freely.

Insects are an important part of the **food chain,** providing tasty meals for other creatures such as bats, birds and other small animals.

It is interesting and fun to keep woodlice, caterpillars, slugs, ladybirds, beetles, worms and many other creatures as pets. What a lot you can learn from them! Watching them eat, sleep, climb, burrow, explore, lay eggs, mate and change into adults while you care for them at home, is exciting: making friends with them is very rewarding.

Keeping Woodlice as Pets is Fun

Woodlice make ideal pets - especially if you have an allergy to furry or feathered pets!

An old fish tank or a large plastic storage box would make an ideal home for woodlice, as they cannot climb easily up smooth surfaces to escape. Put a layer of smooth compost, about 10 - 15 cm deep, in the bottom of the container, as they like to dig quite deeply. Lay some leaf litter on top, and place pieces of wood bark or little stones in the tank, for them to hide under. Their home must not be allowed to dry out, as woodlice need damp conditions. A daily spray with water should be enough to keep the soil moist - but not soggy!

The little creatures will eat the decaying leaf litter, or they can also be fed on tiny pieces of fruit, or vegetable peelings.

Woodlice are quite shy and usually lay their eggs, mate and feed at night-time. They do get used to artificial light, so they are not difficult to observe. It would be a good idea to watch them nearly every day and write a nature diary about their activities.

A Bug Club Competition

If you do keep woodlice or other minibeasts as pets, why not keep a diary and send it in to the Bug Club, run by the Amateur Entomologists' Society (AES). There is a continuing competition that you can enter at any time with details available from the Bug Club email at bug-club@amentsoc.org. If you'd prefer to write in to the AES for competition details or for any other information, including Bug Club membership, you'll find the Society's address on page 31 of this book.

It is very important, before deciding to keep any animal as a pet, that you find out how to look after it correctly and get the permission of a parent or guardian. You could also discuss it with your teacher. Advice and care sheets for many commonly kept minibeasts can be found on the AES website: www.amentsoc.org/insects/caresheets.

WHERE TO GO FOR MORE INFORMATION

As well as finding minibeasts and other insects in the garden and observing them, there are some other important ways you can find out more about these fascinating creatures.

These include books, societies, museums, places to obtain interesting minibeasts and helpful websites.

Books

Your local library will have books on insects and natural history. A good starting point to find out about insects is the following book:

Insects
By George McGavin.
(RSPB Pocket Nature series)
Dorling Kindersley, 2005.
ISBN 978-1-4053-0596-9

A fun book, with insect projects:

Nick Baker's Bug Book
By Nick Baker.
New Holland Publishers, 2002.
ISBN 978-1-8597-4895-4

A book about life in the garden:

What's in your garden?
By Colin Spedding.
Brambleby Books, 2010.
ISBN 978-1-8597-4895-4

Books on popular British insects:

A Year in the Lives of British Ladybirds
By Michael Majerus, Remy Ware and Christina Majerus.
Amateur Entomologists' Society, 2008.
ISBN 978-0-9000-5473-0

British Butterflies Throughout the Year
By Peter May.
Amateur Entomologists' Society, 2007.
ISBN 978-0-9000-5472-3

Societies you can join

There are many local natural history societies you can join. These include:

YOUR COUNTY WILDLIFE TRUST. There are almost 50 county wildlife trusts in Britain, often with their own nature reserves and events.

Wildlife Trusts
The Kiln, Waterside, Mather Road,
Newark, Notts. NG24 1WT.
Tel 01636 677711.
Email: enquiry@wildlifetrusts.org
Website: www.wildlifetrusts.org

OTHER LOCAL SOCIETIES. There are many local entomological societies, or local societies that include insect sections. Examples of well established societies are:

      The Lancashire and Cheshire Entomological Society.

      The Yorkshire Naturalists' Union.

      The Derbyshire and Nottinghamshire Entomological Society.

      The London Natural History Society.

There are also national societies. A good starting point and a gateway into the insect world is:

THE AMATEUR ENTOMOLOGISTS' SOCIETY,
PO Box 8774,
LONDON SW7 5ZG.
Email: tales@amentsoc.org
Website: www.amentsoc.org

This is the society that has published this book, and it has a Bug Club for younger members, which is run in partnership with the Royal Entomological Society.

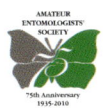  

Museums

Many museums will show you their collections of insects and other invertebrates and often give interesting talks about them.

The Natural History Museum in London has the largest insect collection in the British Isles and is well worth a visit. The museum's new Darwin Centre is especially friendly and will help you to identify and do research into their many collections.

> THE NATURAL HISTORY MUSEUM,
> Cromwell Road, London SW7 5BD.
> Tel: 0207 942 500
> Website: www.nhm.ac.uk

Regional museums with good insect collections include the following:

> OXFORD UNIVERSITY
> MUSEUM OF NATURAL HISTORY,
> Parks Road, Oxford. OX1 3PW.
> Tel: 01865 272 950
> Email: info@oum.ox.ac.uk
> Website: www.oum.ox.ac.uk

Seven spot ladybird.

> THE MANCHESTER MUSEUM,
> Oxford Road, Manchester, M13 9PL.
> Tel: 0161 275 2634
> Website: www.museum.manchester.ac.uk

> WORLD MUSEUM LIVERPOOL,
> William Brown Street, Liverpool. L3 8EN.
> Tel: 0151 478 4393
> Website: www.liverpoolmuseums.org.uk/wml

Many other museums have insect collections.
Ask at your local museum before travelling further afield.

Where to get insects and other minibeasts to keep as pets

Many traders sell fascinating insects and other invertebrates suitable to keep as pets. Some of the most popular are stick insects, but there are many others to choose from. If you send off for a trader's catalogue you can choose from a wide range of minibeasts on offer. Discuss this with your parents or teachers first.

You can also find out about the different types of insect pets available, and how to look after them, on the following website:

www.amentsoc.org/insects/caresheets

The website www.easyinsects.co.uk also provides useful information on looking after a range of insects as pets.

Two reliable suppliers of minibeasts are:

Peruvian black stick insect.

Giant spiny stick insect.

Small Life Supplies
Station Buildings, Station Road, Bottesford,
Notts. NG13 0EB.
Tel: 01949 842446.
Website: www.small-life.co.uk

Virginia Cheeseman
21 Willow Close, Flackwell Heath, High Wycombe,
Bucks. HP10 9LH.
Tel: 01628 522632.
Website: www.virginiacheeseman.co.uk

If you have any further questions or cannot find the pet insect you want, please contact us to ask for help:

The Amateur Entomologists' Society,
PO Box 8774, LONDON SW7 5ZG
Email: tales@amentsoc.org
Website: www.amentsoc.org

Websites

There are many websites that provide information on minibeasts of all kinds. The Amateur Entomologists' Society (AES) website is known to be one of the best for explaining about the various types of insects:

> www.amentsoc.org/insects

The AES website also acts as a gateway to many other websites and places where you can find out more about insects. For example, it has a links directory:

> www.amentsoc.org/links

You can find out more about woodlice from a special website which has been designed for children by the Natural History Museum. It can be found on the Museum's website at:

> www.nhm.ac.uk/woodlice

Time for bed...

ACKNOWLEDGEMENTS

Once again, I should like to thank the Amateur Entomologists' Society, the publishers of this unique 'Faction' Tales & Truths about Garden Minibeasts series for young children. It is an honour for me that the highly regarded entomologists who make up the AES Council of Trustees continue both their commitment to this series and their belief in the value that these books have for small children growing up in a world so overtaken by technology.

Thank you Dafydd Lewis, AES Secretary, who has burnt the candle at both ends to help edit, administer and promote the books, aided and abetted by Dr David Lonsdale, Dr Kieren Pitts and Jacqueline Ruffle, and to Paul Richards for his comments and woodlice images. Thanks also to Dr Robin Wootton, President of the AES, former Registrar Nick Holford and other members of the AES for their enthusiastic support.

Thanks to our illustrator Nick Page for his charming drawings and his perseverance in getting the entomological details in place on the bodies and limbs of each creature. Thanks also to 'Stani' Miles, winner of the Little Green Pig writing competition, for permission to include in this book his poem 'A Woodlouse'.

Warm thanks to Martin Latham, Manager of Waterstone's in Canterbury and his excellent team, especially Janey, for finding space on their children's bookshelves to sell the books; for so kindly describing them as a 'Canterbury sensation' and for launching a successful beetle event in the shop for crowds of enthusiastic youngsters. Likewise to Waterstone's other branch in Rose Lane managed by Richard Hills and his helpful staff.

Other invaluable encouragement came from: Maxwell V.L. Barclay, Head Curator of Coleoptera at the Entomology Department of the Natural History Museum, London; Emma Sherlock, Curator of Lower Invertebrates at the Museum's Department of Zoology, and President of the Earthworm Society of Britain; Simon King, Wildlife Cameraman and TV/Film Presenter and his daughter Savannah (to whom this book is dedicated) and Debbie Cripps, his Promotions Manager; Steve Backshall, Naturalist and Explorer; Dr Martin Warren, Chief Executive of Butterfly Conservation; Professor Stuart R. Harrop, Director of the Durrell Institute of Conservation & Ecology (DICE) and of the School of Anthropology and Conservation, the University of Kent, Canterbury; and Kate Pool of The Society of Authors.

Thanks to Carol Townsend, Head Teacher of St. Peter's Methodist School, Canterbury, and her staff and pupils for their invitation to visit the school and for the warm welcome they gave me and my collection of minibeasts. Similarly to staff and pupils of Langham Primary School in Rutland for their welcome: to Mrs. Suzanne Coughlan, Assistant Head Teacher, Caitlin Price, Luke Baley and Sam Janis for their enthusiastic commendations. And thanks to all the other primary schools requesting visits from me (accompanied by my insects) to talk to their pupils about the books.

I would like to thank the many families, friends, neighbours and everyone else whose encouragement has been most welcome, including Mr and Mrs Paul Eastes and children Caitlin and Beth; Rachel Hubbard, her children George, Rosa, Lauren, Gabriella and Arran; to Amber, Anousca, Yarrick and Bohdi Moubray; to Bernard and Victoria Miles; Bob and Fran Peet and their granddaughter Emily.

Very special thanks once again to Darren Gander, of Darren Gander Graphic Design, for working his artistic magic with such goodwill on the cover, page designs and the publicity pages. Similarly to the team in the University of Kent's Print Office, including Ian White, Nick Page, Marion Smith and Damon Woods.

Thank you to my best friend Carole Fries for her continuing support, likewise to dear friends Sir Frank Barlow, Stella Irwin, Janice Booth Carver, Monty Chisholm, Jacqueline De B. Hovell and Albert Bullock.

To my fantastic children, Samantha and Orlando - thank you for putting up with my passion and being nice to the insects. Last but not least, warm thanks to Charles Warren Lord, the most patient of partners and for the commendation from his sons, Martin and Peter.

Finally, this book is dedicated to Betty Copeland, my mother, who sadly died on 17th April 2010 and who would have been delighted to know it was sponsored by her legacy.   *Sonia Copeland Bloom.*

More photographs of woodlice with their entomological names; from left to right working down the page:
1. *Armadillidium vulgare*.; 2. A *trichoniscid*; 3. *Porcellio scaber*.
4. *Philoscia muscorum*; 5. *Oniscus asellus*; 6. *Porcellio scaber*.
7. *Ligea oceanica*; 8. *Trichoniscoides sarsi*; 9. *Armadillidium depressum*.
10. *Platyarthrus hoffmannseggi*; 11. *Armadillidium vulgare*; 12. *Porcellio spinicornis*.
13. *Oniscus asellus* and *Dysdera* spp.; 14. *Androniscus dentiger*.